HECKINGTON
1999

THE WAY WE ARE

By
Pat Banister
&
Mary Wilkinson

Printed by
Wayzgoose
Sleaford.

All rights reserved. Reproduction by any means including photocopying, or storage in any retrieval system whether mechanical, electric, electronic, or by photoelectric or other means without prior written permission of the copyright holders or the copyright holder's assigns or successors in title is strictly forbidden except for the purpose of comment or review.

Copyright 1999
P.Banister & M.Wilkinson.

ISBN 0 9535362 0 3

Published by
Curlynegs Publishing
Heckington, Sleaford,
Lincolnshire.

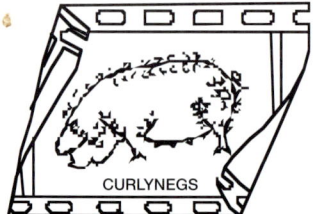

ACKNOWLEDGEMENTS

We would like to express our grateful thanks to all those who have helped in any way in the compilation and preparation of this book including:
Mr Charles Raphael for his computer knowledge and expertise, without his valuable help we should still be wandering in the wilderness. Retired Heckington schoolteacher Mrs Woods, Retired Pearoom worker Mrs Zealand, Mr Harold Lowth, Mr Ron Lowth, Mr &Mrs Aldhouse, Mr & Mrs Howett. Old Heckingtonian Mr Walter Cook, Mr Don Enderby, Miss B.D.Denman, Mr Roy Denman. Churchwardens Micheal Cullen and Barry Young. The reverend David Boutle for his help in accessing and photographing the Church and Mr Roy Sumner for photographs and information.
To all those who allowed us to advertise on their premises:
To Mrs Eve Hannell for her help in securing orders.
To Beth Davidson and North Kesteven District Council photographic archives and also the use of their computer file compression hardware.
To Heckington Village Trust for historical information and the use of display equipment.
To all those who allowed us to disrupt their daily routine by taking up their valuable time and asking them to pose for us and to anyone who has helped in any way.
Finaly to our respective spouses who have patiently put up with us eating, sleeping and talking of nothing but photography and this book for the last twelve months. Without the help and support of all these people this publication would not have been possible.

INTRODUCTION

We make no apology for putting the Christian places of worship first in this book even though the rest is in alphabetical order. It is only through the influence of the Christian belief that our years are numbered as they are. Therefore only because of that, this year is counted as 1999. There are many millions of people in the world to whom the year 2,000 means nothing at all.

Heckington has a long and historic past, which over the years has been recorded in various forms. Mostly this has had to be the written word with the exception of a few drawings, paintings and lithographs. It was the advent of the camera in the 1840s that really gave us the means to look back at how it used to be. All over the country there were men and women who saw the exciting potential of this new form of art. One such person was Micheal Cole Sumners who came to settle in the village from Folkingham in 1864 bringing his camera with him. Having visited here in 1860 and taken photographs of the High Street and Church Street. So, as far as can be ascertained it was he who began the photographic record of Heckington. These pictures have survived and together with many other photographers such as Ben Smith in the 30s and 40s and Irene Zealand from the 50s to the present day have created the images of the past that we have to look back on. We are attempting to carry on that tradition.

It was our intention to create a commemorative record of the village during this last year of the 1900s so that in a few years time others or we can look back at how it was. Many of us enjoy a nostalgic look into the past. To create this atmosphere we have included some photographs taken of Heckington in years gone by. These are paired with the same shot taken this year to compare the changes that have taken place. There are images of buildings and streets with people at work and leisure. It is by no means a complete record, to do that would require a book of hundreds of pages and the cost would be prohibitive. However we hope it will give a 'taste' of life in our village as we approach the end of the twentieth century.

PB & MW.

The magnificent Church of Saint Andrew apropriated by the monks of Bardney Abbey in 1345 although building work had begun before then. It is thought to be the third church to occupy the site.

The imposing stone and brick design of the Methodist Church. Built in 1905 with one of the new lime trees planted in 1996 in the foreground on Church street.

The Wesleyan Reform chapel in Eastgate with its datestone of 1858.

The impressive victorian cemetery chapels designed by Richard Almond of Palace Chambers Westminster in 1879. Currently under restoration by the parish council the bell, badly cracked and unsafe has been removed hopefully to be recast.

The row of cottages in Bank's Lane with its unsurfaced road.

Bank's Lane today still with the cottages but a clean metalled road and looking a lot more friendly and inviting.

Dennis Mason and Daniel Wilkinson at Heckington Supplies, Hazelwoods Yard, Boston Road.

Osbourne Way off Godson Avenue, a pleasant retirement close, not to far away from the village shops.

Once a busy family run general store on the Boston Road.

Now almost unrecognisable as a private house.

Looking towards the village frome the cemetery on Boston Road. The large house on the right was used by the military during WW2 and the large tree in the left foreground is one of a pair of giant Wellingtonia that stood at the cemetery gates.

Today the trees and hedge have grown considerably and are about to suffer a mechanical trim. The road looks in better condition and footways have been constructed. The magnificent Wellingtonias have long been felled.

The proud owner standing outside the shop in the High Street where the Co-Op supermarket now stands.

The Pinfold, once used to enclose stray cattle, now planted as a herb garden, and looked after by Tony Conn, the seat was given by the Garden Club in memory of their treasurer, Mrs Hazel Palmer who died in 1994 and is missed by all her friends.

The quiet residential area that is Bramley Close.

Approaching Heckington along the Burton Road. The railway crossing and the Church can be seen in the distance.

Cameron Street, once Saint Andrew's Street at its junction with Church Street in the 1920s.

The same view today. The cottages in the foreground have gone together with the bicycle delivery boy. The sunshades on Turnell's butchers shop mark out the building that was once also the Red Cow inn.

Greenacres, Cameron Street, Heckingtons Residential Home for the elderly, allows locals to remain close to their families and friends.

A quiet cul-de-sac of starter homes near the railway line off Burton Road.

Eager and excited children wait outside the Methodist Church to embark on the annual singing round the village.

A Garden Party for the young at Sally and Charles Pinchbecks, Cowgate.
The Explorers and friends meet at the Methodist Chapel each Sunday morning.
Freya Gwinnett, Sally Pinchbeck, Alice Pinchbeck, Alice Hayler, Chloe Gwinnett,
Fiona Gwinett with baby Robert Gwinnett.

Chapel Garden Party. Looking after the cake stall and raffle, Margaret Boultbee, Thomas Pinchbeck, Charles Pinchbeck, Jean Louth, Chris Mitchell

With C.Pinchbeck's cottage on the left and the Gasworks on the corner where 'Fourways' the bungalow at 22 Cowgate now stands.

Barry Taylor well known to locals as postman and football coach to the youngsters. Alan Wilkinson receiving the mail, and passing the time of day.

Christopher Close, plenty of space and mature trees make it a very pleasant area to live. Close to shops, school, and Playing field, newer estates have less room than these built 20 years ago.

Church Street with its thatched cottages, children playing, and a gathering of local tradesmen. This picture was taken in 1860 before the restoration of the pitched roof on the Church in 1867.

A lot more traffic now. The village pump has been replaced by the village crest and the trees have been replanted behind the railings.

The mobile Midland Bank, if you blink you will miss it.

At the end of Church Street the entrance to the Manor, to the left a house built in 1828, used to be called the Black house years ago, as it was covered with a black substance which still remains on the back of the house today.

Ray and Sue Perry with Pat Bentley outside the corner shop on Chuch Street. Newsagent, groceries, wines and spirits, makes this a busy shop, but always service with a smile

The first Saturday in the month and the refuse truck parks at the corner of Churchill Way. A large house was demolished in the early 60s to make way for the road and a thatched cottage stood where the rendered wall is now.

The barbers and the Six Bells pub on Church Street. The postmans uniform has changed a bit since then.

There is still a hairdresser on the site. Pictured is owner Ginny Simpson who took over in 1979, with her assistant Tracy Kay. However the pub has given way to a ladies outfitters owned by chairman of the parish council Jan Palmer here with Charlotte Sim.

These properties on Church Street have seen many changes, what sort of shop was the one with the large window I wonder, and when did it stop being a shop?

The Manor, once owned by the Godson Family, is now an alcholic rehabilitation clinic,once a childrens home ,and then a home for the elderly. The protrusion on the roof is part of the lift system that was installed many years ago.

Alan and Rosemary Stoker have been looking after the fruit and vegatables since 1985, and also have a huge selection of fancy goods. Thier window is always dressed imaginatively and catches the eye of those passing through.

Reverand David Boutle on his way to prepare for a wedding, the photographers are getting set up for the arrival of the first guests.

On the corner of Churchill Way in the last year of the 1900s Heckington still only has a trailer library visiting on two days a week. Local librarian Helen Hill is standing in the doorway always on hand to help.

Houses and roads still under construction on the corner of Coleby Way.

The Co-op is still the largest shop for groceries in the village, and is very important for those without transport. Customer Bernadette Clifton and Julie Simpson.

The co-op has many assistants, here is Karen Moore and Sue Rudden.

The old Co-op shop down the High Street. The mini car hadn't been out long when this picture was taken. Fray Bentos corned beef was 3/11d or 20p in todays money.

Only the archway remains today to remind us of where it was.

Sports day on a summers afternoon at the new school on Howell Road. The school has grown as the new houses have been built, and now has an extra classroom added on, and will soon need more space as the village continues to grow.

The Royal Oak at the Cross Roads, on fine days customers enjoy sitting out on the front watching the world go by.

The blacksmith's (Cook's) corner in days gone by. L to R, Walter Lowth (smith & farrier) Walter Cook Snr, Unknown apprentice, Frank Cook as a child (elder brother of Walter Cook of Heckington Magazine fame) & grandfather Billy Cook.

Today the buildings are unchanged. There are motor cars in the yard instead of horsedrawn implements. The framework in the foreground is the cricket club sight screen in for an overhaul.

A leasurly afternoon in Edwardian times looking down Eastgate from the Cross-roads. The public water standpipe can be seen centre foreground The large stone that the young boy is sitting on was to stop waggons fouling the wall.

The same view today with the old Royal Oak gone and a busy crossroads. The third building on the right is the council chambers.

Local recycling contractor Mr Ian Sheppard waits patiently at the busy crossroads.

The Crossroads is always busy, the lorries get bigger year on year as the processing plants get larger, many locals are employed by these local firms.

Peter Asher well known local farmer taking advantage of a fine Sunday morning to harvest his wheat on the Sleaford Road.

Farmer Nick Loweth grows asparagus, my favourite vegatable, and can be seen here with some trimmed and washed ready for delivery.

Den Smith hurrying to harvest a load of early potatoes ready for the lorry coming to take them to market.

Michael and Eddy Cullen with a new venture, quality free range eggs, the demand is growing now the trend is away from battery hens.

Probably the final official parade of the Arnhem Veterans, stationed in the village during the second world war, and fondly remembered by many of the locals.

Mrs Karen Barry with her pre-school children and helpers. Most village children enjoy going to a pre-school group prior to starting primary school at five.

Foster Street

Approaching the village from Great Hale with the Millview estate on the right

1

2

3

Heckington Luncheon Club.

Key to pictures on page 96

4

5

6

Ex pupils of Heckington School at their annual reunion held at The Royal Oak on the first wednesday in June every year. (See list of names on last pages).

Heckington Luncheon Club Helpers,
Janet Brandreth, Pat Tremlett, Alma Wilson, Jean Howell, Sheila Grossmith
Agnes Barnard, Chris Hinds

The 2nd Heckington Scouts, Cubs and Beavers with their adult supervisors at a summer event on the playing fields. (See last pages for index of names).

The pleasant well kept gardens of the retirement bungalows in Handley Street. Until the early 70s this was the site of the early post war prefabricated bungalows. (The prefabs).

Bowls is played by many people locally, the day I took this picture there were 73 ladies taking part The green is tucked away behind the Nags Head Pub.

Mrs Heather Wright proprietor of Pet Supplies since May 1992
There is plenty of choice here for all our pets, food, bedding, leads, etc.

Eastgate looking towards the old school, which is now used by Heritage Lincs. The wall on the left has recently been built. Cycling is still a favourite method of exercise and of getting around the village to do the shopping.

Mrs Sue Purnell
Allsorts Party Goods
Parties can be arranged, and all the varies things required can be supplied to make light work of any party organizing. A large choice of toys are also available.

Mrs Irhajamani Aroonachellum with a customer Mrs Brenda Cubitt, the only baker now, but I'm sure some folks remember when there were many more.

Dr. and Mrs K. Brandreth lived here for many years. Surgeries were held here before the new centre on the Sleaford Road was built in 1988.

The bank opens a few hours twice a week and is much appreciated, the post on the pavement in front of the bank however rather spoils the view.

A veiw from the Church over Christopher Close to the new houses shows how the density has increased over the last 20 years.
These are built by Warrington Builders and Developers

The gentleman that started it all. Mr Micheal Cole Sumners standing at the door of his shop which was then also the Post Office. See the letter box to the right under the shop window. Next door was then a plumbers and glaziers.

The Chemists today with, from the left Mrs Jo Marriott, Mrs Karen Clare, Mrs Mary Hulse proprietor Mrs Ruth Bailey, Mrs Jo Marshall . A visit to this chemist is always a pleasure, advice and a chat and lovely things to buy.

Looking southwards from the Church tower to the mill shows how the trees have grown up over the years.

The house farthest away was once a work house, then a public house, now a domestic house. It was the White Horse Inn until 1990, leaving the village with just two public houses now, when once there were eight.

Mrs L Donaldson amongst her enormous assortment of useful things, hardware to help the DIY person, wool and patterns, tools, kitchenware, and much more.

Harvest Insurance Services. 21-23 High Street
Phillip Handford Rod Handford Proprietor Karen Rowan Karen Murrell Viv Wardell

Mandy Katy and Andrew Key

Heckington Newsmart, with proprietors Peter and Janice Hill. They have a wonderful variety of things to offer, hot snacks to take away, papers, stationery, toys, sweets, and are also agents for the National Lottery

One of the earliest known photographs of the High Street taked by Micheal Cole Sumners in 1860. There seem to be several 'important' people about.

Less people about now than then although it's hardly an occasion now when anyone walks down the street with a camera.

The Nags Head has recently been repaired and tidied, and looks fresh once more. Visitors enjoy a break here, on their way to the east coast.

This is now a Veterinary Branch Surgery. Next door is the Squash Club. Veterinary Surgeon Colin Cumming BVM&S MRCVS has his main surgery in Sleaford.

The Elm Holt, once known as The Park. The lady in the picture is Mrs Kate Denman mother of Roy and Miss B.D.Denman. She was 18 years old at the time and just happened to be walking through as the photographer took the picture in 1904.

Many dog walkers will recognise this charming cottage on the old Howell Road.

The Annual Parish Council Meeting in the Village Hall.
Chairman Jan Palmer seen here conferring with the Parish Clerk Trevor Page,
Martin Pocklington, Pat Banister, Harry Grossmith, Mary Wilkinson.
(Pat and Mary authors of this book).

Some of the villagers attending the meeting.

The Village Hall is used by numerous organisations, and has been well looked after over the years. It was built by Mosses Franks in 1863 as a Temperance Hall. What would he think if he came back to-day when the bar was in full swing?

The High Street can get pretty busy these days when both sides of the road are used for parking cars, but it is still better than when the A17 came roaring through.

Looking towards the village from the Pinfold with Limetree Walk on the right just before the house with the interesting roof.

Houlden Way named after a well known local family who once owned and farmed the land. The trees in the distance back on to the Playing Fields.

A view south from the Church tower. Taken before the Methodist chapel was built in 1905. Before the first world war, hence no war memorial.

The same view from the tower now with a car park on the Green and a busy Church Street.

Aerial photograph of the village taken at 11.30am on Sunday 12th September.

These houses on Howell road were council built in 1919, now mostly privately owned, they have an unusual dampcourse made of slate.

Mr and Mrs K Howitt, live in a typical mid 50s style bungalow.

Once Cowgate, now called Kyme Road with the Elm Holt entrance on the left near the trees.

Only the chimneys identify the cottages on the left with electricity replacing the gas light on the corner.

The Elm Holt. Once called The Park and a place of recreation stretching into what is now the Foster Street Estate.

Still a footpath through on the right but all the parkland has gone.

No English village should be without its Fish and Chip shop. The one in Kyme Road stands on its own at present, I wonder when this corner of the village will be filled with houses?

More houses under construction off Lambourne Way.

Above Latimer House with houses in the once much admired gardens to the rear.

Below George a cheerful face as ever, with plenty of news to impart as he goes about his work cleaning windows.

Village Caretaker Mr Micheal Lowth in charge of the big mean sweeping machine.

Mr Roy Denman, well known retired local farmer leans on his scythe for a well earned rest as he mows out the dyke down the Howell Road.

Above. A favourite spot to enjoy the ice cream and pop on sale at the corner shop.

Left. Second world war veteran. Retired Mr Sid Pierce prepares to take a friends dog for a bit of exercise.

Barbara Mansfield, Warden at Willow Close community centre, chatting to Mr. R Sumners on the day he visited with a book of historical records from his family archives.

Ted and Kath Lord enjoying a browse at Mr. Pell's garage sale.

Hazelwoods Yard with John Mann's lorries parked ready for the next consignment to go to Europe

New Street looking from Bank's Lane footpath towards Station Road. The story goes that the row of houses on the left were built by a man that had fallen out with the doctor, to spoil his view across the countryside.

Sleaford Road as it was up to the early 70s with both a pub and a garage. The next building past the pub was the cobblers.

Sleaford Road now. Almost unrecognisable except for the Red House garden wall in the left foreground and the house with the double pitch roof in the distance.

The thriving community of families that was once Newton's Yard Lane.

Today almost unrecognisable, except for the house in the distance at the junction with Church Street.

Old whitewashed cottages with roses in the garden and the 'New' Royal Oak in the background.

Now a car park but the old garden fence betrays its past history.

The cottages on the old school corner as it was up to the early 60s.

Now with its pleasant green, seat and Silver Birch trees planted by the Village Trust in 1973.

Barry Young churchwarden for ten years and county councillor from May this year looks out thoughtfuly across the village from the Church tower.

Paul Tarry village postmaster, parish councillor and school governor takes a breath of air before the morning rush.

The Post Office corner when the horse and bicycle ruled the road and the smell of freshly baked bread came from next door. The three storey Red House has been involved with schooling several times in the past.

The view has changed little except the bakers is now a restaurant and the road is covered in yellow and white lines to control the motor car. The Red House is still involved with childrens schooling.

Still at the Post Office corner this house stood on the corner of Bank's Lane. It was a private school in the 1870s. Photographs needed long exposures in those days thus the 'ghost' of the dog on the corner. It moved before the exposure was completed.

Jubilee Terrace now stands on the corner. Opposite is the shop once owned by tinker Lupton. Now Donaldson's DIY selling almost everything you might need to make or mend around the house.

Chapel Street with its gas lights, the Adult School and May Jones' shop on the left and the gates to the Hall in the distance

Now called Saint Andrew's Street and the building on the left converted into flats. The house on the right looks as if it managed to hold on to its iron railings throughout the war.

The village pond on the junction of Sleaford Road and Boston Road. The 'other' mill can be seen in the background. The round thatched cottage on the right was painted with black gas tar and was known as The Inkpot.

Modern development and the bus shelter occupy the same spot today with the pond filled in and grassed over.

The old mill on the Sleaford Road. Once a busy hive of industry. The horse and waggon look as if they have been brought to take away a load.

Below,
Now looking rather forlorn. Perhaps waiting for someone to give it a new lease of life?

Sleaford Road, approaching Burton Road junction with the water tower still standing and the road showing clear signs of the number of horses using it.

The same view today. Note how the road and footway have been built up by counting the courses of bricks visible in garden wall on the right.

The last village Bobby. PC Powell on his final day and closing the village office. Due no doubt to lack of rescources and investment into the Lincolnshire Force.

After a transitional spell in portacabins in the car park patients of the Heckington Medical Practice were able to enjoy the new facilities. It was opened on the 29th January 1988 by Professor V.W.M Drury the president of the Royal College of General Practitioners.

Tom Walker standing at the entrance to his newly modernised vehicle servicing business. Next door is the forecourt of Mr Arthur Scoggins car sales. A well known local businessman who, sadly, at the age of 82 died in September.

The neat row of terraced cottages in Saint Andrew's Street.

The evening rush of children arriving home from the Sleaford schools by train.

I wonder if like us these young ladies will view their current fashion of clothes in quite the same light in twenty or thirty years time.

The quiet leafy lane that was once Station Road.

Today all the trees are gone with only the railings left and Mr Pell busy tending his garden.

Looking from the crossroads towards the mill with Wellington Close to the left and the remaining large tree in the centre.

Alan and Rosemary Creaser in front of their home which is one of the few larger non estate houses to be built in recent years.

The smiling faces of the pea sorters at the Pearoom in the early 60s. From L to R; Mrs Parkinson, Mrs Long, Mrs V. Bailey, Mrs E.Lowth, Mrs Woodcock, Mr H.Lowth, Mr F.Hewardine, Mrs Jeffries, Mrs Duncan, Mrs G. Todkill.

The same operation being carried out by one person in the ultra clean stainless steel environment of one of Mr J.L.Priestly's food processing factories on the Station Road industrial site.

The Pearoom seen from the Station. The Victorian waiting rooms now house a Railway museum run by the Village Trust.

Heckington Station looking clean and tidy, few trains pass these days but it is a very important service for connecting to the main line at Grantham, also to Lincoln from Sleaford and on into the Midlands.

The once busy Railway Hotel with stabling close to the mill, Pearoom and station.

Today a private house with Mrs Val Bristow and her grandchildren caught passing on a sunny summers day walk.

One of the original alms houses on the Green the other having been burnt down a few years before. To the left of this in front of the corner shop stood the village stocks. Part of the Church still has a flat roof. This dates the picture at 1886/7 when the roof was restored to a pitched one.

Now well established among the trees are the new Alms Houses financed by Mr Henry Godson a local benefactor. Half of the Green now having succumbed to the motor car.

This shot was taken standing next to the corner shop mentioned opposite. The trees look to have been recently pollarded.

This shot taken from roughly the same spot as the finishing touches are put to construction in readiness for the nights crowds.

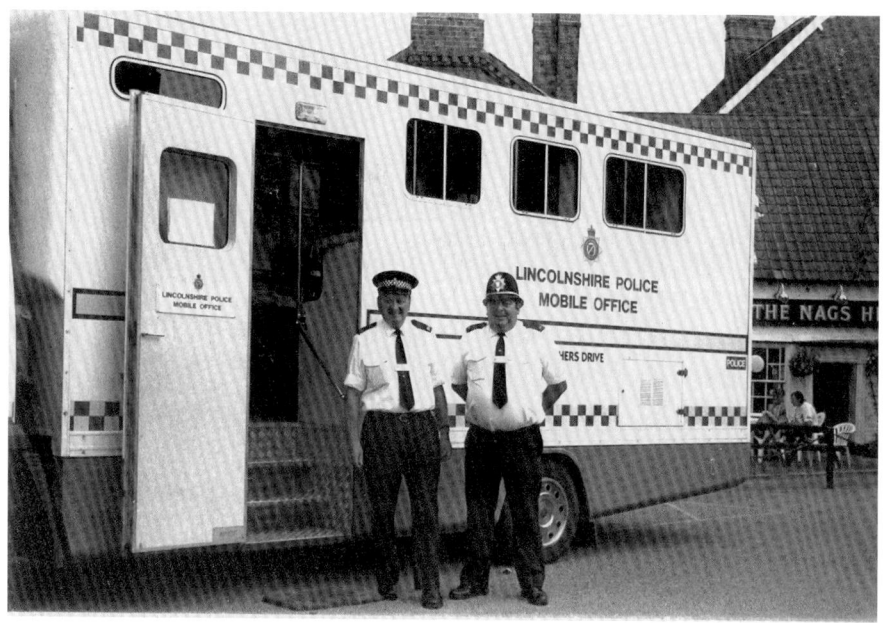

In the absence of a village constable and a police office we now have an occasional visit from the mobile station. Pictured are two of the helpful smiling officers in attendance.

Some of the crowd of visitors to one of the exhibition tents at this years Heckington Show. The person on the left in the dark glasses is Mrs Margaret Banister.

One of the best loved and oldest of the attractions at the Show is the cycle racing. Thanks to the care and maintenance by the hard working members of the committee the racing circuit attracts riders from all over the country.

Another popular event is the gruelling ten mile road race run from the stadium around the fens and back. Number 77 is local Heckington man Simon Bell who finished second.

Mrs Nickols takes Heckington Show competition entries in the marquee.

Prizewinners entrants and officials at the Playing field Sports Club's tenth annual vegetable show. L To R; M.A.Banister, D.Woods-Thorpe, R.Massingham, V.Bristow, D.Enderby, K.Woods-Thorpe, C.Baxter, A.Bristow, R.Bristow, F.Bourne, L.Bristow.

John Knight outside his shop in Vicarage Road. He is the 3rd generation of the same family to own it. His grandfather took it over from Kirtons in 1945. They in turn had taken it over from Tailbys. A butchers having occupied the site for at least a hundred years.

Mr George Knight with his new van in 1946.

A group of Edwardian children on the footpath through Newton's Yard to Church Street.

Today, although the footpath is still there the open fields have given way to housing developement.

Viewed from the Church tower the footpath is now enclosed between the lapboard fence in the left foreground. To the left is the Churchill Way estate. To the right the houses of Osbourne Way.

Surely a good advertisement for the quality of houses is when the developer lives in one of them. The fine property on the right is where he lives at the entrance to Wellington Close

The view seen by countless newly weds over the years as they turn to walk back down the aisle. Perhaps to return a few years later for their children to be baptised at the font.

The impressive wooden pulpit with it's highly polished brass handrail must have witnessed many a change in the style of sermon delivered.

The elegant organ was restored and moved to this position many years ago. Once having to be pumped by hand the bellows to supply the air have for many years now been powered by electricity.

No photograph whether black and white or colour can possibly do justice to the magnificent stained glass in Heckington Church. It has to be seen in reality.

This window can be found to the left of the alter.

Finally to the event of the 11th August this year. A view of the eclipse as you might have seen it had you been in the vicinity of the mill.

Luncheon Club
1. Mrs K Waltham, Mr. J Duncalf, Mrs M Young, Mrs I Colbourne, Mrs M Gash
2. Mrs P Musson, Mrs D Rudkin, Mrs J Neaverson, Mr D Neaverson, Mrs L Darnell, Mr K Musson, Mrs D Scriven
Single Pictures Mrs M B Trevitt, Mrs P Stevenson
3. Mr D Neaverson, Mrs L Darnell, Mrs P Musson, Mrs D Ruskin, Mrs D Neaverson, Mrs J Barnatt, Mrs M Walters
4. Mrs J Hollingsworth, Mrs M Clark, Mrs J Sweeney, Mr N Hollingsworth
5. Mrs J Corley, Mr R Colby
6. Mrs M Whitfield, Mr G Stubley, Mr R Watts

BACK COVER
No book on Heckington would be complete without a picture of the majestic eight sailed mill. It is open regularly to the public and wholemeal flour is ground by the Friends of the Mill.

Key to school reunion.

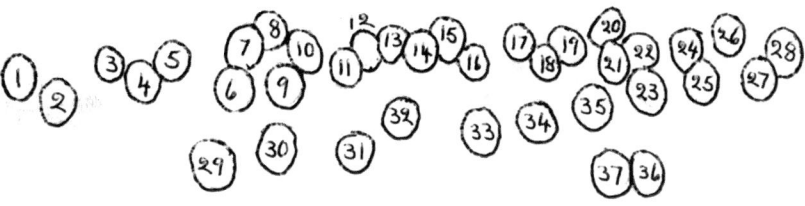

(1) Norman Clark, (2) Audry Taylor, (3) Tony Garner, (4) Colin Crop, (5) Gordon Howles, (6) Miss B.Denman, (7) Ray Bell, (8) Gerald Levesley, (9) Jill Hatcliff, (10) Gordon Hatcliff, (11) Maurice Humberstone, (12) Harry Bowden, (13) Norman Pell, (14) Sid Hinton, (15) Harry Gresham, (16) Ron Star, (17) Reg Star, (18) Richard Mowbery, (19) Gordon Smalley, (20) Charles Mowbery, (21) Don Enderby, (22) Roy Pell, (23) Arthur Horn, (24) Lewis Pell, (25) Betty Rooney, (26) Ron Lowth, (27) Geoff Young, (28) George Dobbs, (29) Eileen Stanley, (30) Leila Bembridge, (31) May Woods, (32) Brian Hubbert, (33) Norman Blow, (34) Peggy Wetton, (35) Margaret Woods, (36) Elsie Archer, (37) Eve Hannell.
The annual event is organised by Mrs E. Hannell nee Smalley. Old Heckingtonians have attended from as far away as Australia.

Index to the 2nd Heckington Scouts, Cubs and Beavers.
Standing at rear
Mr Tim Grigg Cub scout leader, Mr Bruce Lyon Scout leader, Miss Kate Frost Beaver scout leader, Mrs Liz Peto Group Scout leader, Mr Micheal Wells Assistant Cub scout leader.
Back row Scouts
James Richardson, Craig Twell, Thomas Barr, Alice Peto, Kelly Lyon, Joe Peto, Guy Sear, Ali-Tom Frost, Mathew Hill.
Middle Row Cubs
Tom Baxter, Sean Mason, Aston Hodgson, Scott Norris, Robert Barr, Nicholas Higgs, Micheal Wells jr, Stuart Graham, Andrew Wells, Jack Musson, James Grigg, Christopher Baldwin.
Front row Beavers
Joshua Wells, Andrew Baldwin, Micheal South, Thomas Pinchbeck, Guy Bailey, Ryan Norris, James Clark, Fredrick Bell, Johnathan Higgs, Daniel Lyon, Ben Stocks.

NOTES